Look at the Lake

By the same author:

Look at the Lake

Kevin Brophy

PUNCHER & WATTMANN

First published in 2018
Published by Puncher and Wattmann
PO Box 441
Glebe NSW 2037

http://www.puncherandwattmann.com
puncherandwattmann@bigpond.com

National Library of Australia
Cataloguing-in-Publication entry:

Brophy, Kevin

Look at the Lake

ISBN   9781925780086

I. Title.

A821.3

Cover design by David Musgrave, photograph courtesy of the author

Printed by Lightning Source International

This book was supported by a publication grant from the University of Melbourne

This project has been assisted by the Australian Government through the Australia Council, its arts funding and advisory body.

Contents

This book is dedicated to my parents, Leo Brophy (1920-2017) and Moria Brophy (née Hutton 1924-2017), who both died while Andrea and I were away in the desert, though both of them urged us to go and they both had a strong interest in all we were doing there. My thanks and love to them for this.

'Look at the lake. It is shaped like a heart.'
Hanson Pye, *Desert Lake* (CSIRO, 2013)

Introduction

These poems were written across one year, mostly at the rate of a poem a day. The year was 2016. I spent most of that year in the remote Aboriginal community of Mulan on the edge of the Great Sandy Desert of Western Australia. As a volunteer at the local school, as a newcomer to the Kimberley, and as a visitor to this community, I had a lot of learning to do, and many new impressions to record.

The following is a selection of those poems written in 2016, revised in hindsight, and discussed with the elders of the Mulan community. Some of the poems were commissioned by members of the community once they became aware I was recording my experiences while living with them.

Mulan is home to the traditional Walmajarri speaking custodians of the Indigenous Protected Area (IPA) around Lake Paruku (Lake Gregory on many maps). These people have known this land along with its stories, songs and rituals for a very long time, certainly for more than 40,000 years. In the dry season people visit the many important traditional sites around the lake, and they fire the red sand spinifex country during their hunting time. They still make use of the seasonal fruits, plants and vegetables in this semi-arid desert. Art is important to the community, as is Australian Rules Football, music, and the education of children in the local school. Such a remote community of less than two hundred people with so few resources and such extreme conditions faces almost insurmountable problems related to isolation, ill-health, poverty, low life expectancy, under employment, and a lack of education. Against this, the people in the Mulan community have their home and identity in this land, and most importantly an enduring knowledge and connection with their environment in all its moods and aspects.

Sometimes the poems are portraits or stories, sometimes they are incidents that I thought were vivid accounts of life here, or somehow important to record; sometimes they are the kinds of things an outsider notices. Most often, they are the reactions of a poet to the large and small human moments encountered in any community. The poems are meant to be respectful and affectionate towards the place, the traditions and the people of Mulan who have been so kind to let me live here for the last two years. Many of the poems were inspired by being with the children of Mulan at the John Pujajangka-Piyirn Catholic School. I am grateful for the chance to work with these children and to get to know them.

My particular thanks and gratitude for friendship, tolerance and honesty go to Veronica Karnpirr Lulu, Noonie Elizabeth Lulu, Karen Lulu, Jarvis Fernandez, Bessie Doonday, Shirley Yoomarie, Steven and Julie Yoomarie, Eileen Tax, Shirley Brown, Jamie Brown, Lenny Boxer, Wendy Burn, and the children of the school who are soon to become the men and women leading their community.

The poems are mostly written in free verse, which means that each poem seeks its own rhythm and its own line lengths, usually with an ear out for how it might be read aloud or perceived on the page. Not all these poems are fully formed. Some are closer to jotted notes, some are half-realised thoughts, but each one adds an aspect to the experience of a year spent rapidly recording impressions, and pressing these into language that aims to speak vividly, originally and honestly. This project of imposing the poet's eye on what was to me a new world, kept me watching and kept me thinking and it kept me feeling my way through that year.

I am thankful to have shared this experience with my partner, Andrea who inspired me, opened me up to new ways of thinking, and kept me going.

Through the dramas and landscapes we encountered, through sharing the place with our occasional much loved visitors, and with the widening group of people in Mulan we came to know and value, we have been privileged and lucky.

My thanks for reading, encouragement, forbearance and inspiration to 'Salon 16': Myron Lysenko, Kate Ahearne , Sally Pridgeon , Lyndon Walker, Tracey McGuire, Angela Gash, Lynn Davidson, Nadia Niaz, Gayelene Carbis, Andrea Lloyd , Gabi Bridge, Sophie Lloyd, Katia Ariel, Wendy Haslem, Pam Lloyd, Robyn Martinez, Peter Russo, Liz MacFarlane, Margaret Lloyd, Francesca Manca, Vin Martin, Cathie McCormick and Patten Bridge. Without you the poems could not have found a voice. In the course of the year you saw so many more poems than the ones appearing in this book, and you were gracious to give them your attention. This book is a partial reflection of the path you took with me in 2016.

Thanks to Bruce for that trip down the Canning Stock Route, and to Tony for the trips between Mulan and Balgo, and for stories around our fires.

My further heartfelt thanks to John Leonard for his final help in shaping this book, and to David Musgrave and Ann Vickery for showing enough confidence in the project to publish these poems.

Small discoveries along the way: the names brolga, witchetty and corella are all remnants of languages lost. There are many hundreds of types of Christmas Beetles, all of them remarkable. Both the land and the people sicken if they cannot be near each other often enough. The lake knows when its people have returned to it. The children know the taste of nearly every creature in their environment.

A Map

for Susan Hampton

The first thing people will do
is sprinkle the map with sand,
she said.
Three fingers pulled through the sand
might mean there's water here
but only in winter.
Two fingers under this might show
that birds rest here
and you might catch one
and eat it
if you're quick and lucky.
On this map
old women might sing Christian songs
in voices more ancient than their faces.
We find our souls are in our laps
when we open a map
and lean over its expanse.
A finger like a bird of prey
casts its shadow on the open road,
lake, town.
The map never folds away
as neatly as it arrived, for its
soul, swollen a little with longing
to be known
wants to stay open on our laps.

Rice Puffs, Pringles, Lindt

We shop
as if the apocalypse
is scheduled for next week.
And perhaps it is.
Tinned food by the boxful,
everyone grabbing water,
breakfast cereal, energy bars.
Chocolate's always on special;
and ice—everyone needs bags of it.
The chilled meat looks freshly
torn from panicked creatures.
Everyone concentrates.
Ready to pounce on any long-lastings.

Dusty four-wheel drives
cough sand and smoke outside
hunched in on themselves
dreaming of some long stretch
of rotting road to a safe place
where the worst disaster
would be running out of water,
toilet rolls, Rice Puffs, Pringles, Lindt.

Camel

All nose, teeth, knees and attitude,
it walks as if taught to do it in a world far from here
where walking might be the point of living
and eyelashes for no good reason
have become elaborate reedy shades
over eyes lapping with a dark liquid knowledge.
Again and again its half-inflated feet come down
soft and inquiring upon the sand.
If you could, you would choose such a creature
to deliver a gift.

Mulan to Balgo and Back to Mulan

Do you want to come with me today
in the old Toyota
on the broken track to Balgo
to pick up another old Toyota
to drive back
and find the car is missing
when we get there,
and then do you want to come
to the canyon
on an even more broken track
looking for the old Toyota
out at the big dam, way past
the cliffs with a cave
where a nun is said to have lived
for years,
and find when we get to
the big dam
under a sky of swirling eagles
that the old Toyota isn't there,
and then do you want to come
back with me to the town of Balgo
and drive out to a waterfall,
picking up some kids along the way
out for a walk in the desert,
to find when we get to that waterfall
that the old Toyota was there but
has gone now back to Balgo,
and do you want to come back to Balgo
with me again then
and once we find
that old Toyota there,

do you want to drive it back
down the busted road to Mulan behind me?
It will help to break up your day.

Ian, Brian, Yvette, Kenny and the Ride-on Mower

Ian shows us the frozen scorpion and spider
kept at the back of the shop.
Brian says the scorpion could kill
a small school boy.
Yvette shows us yesterday's photo,
a millipede that turns out to be a centipede
but it could paralyse you anyway.
The ride-on mower stalls at the barbed wire
and Kenny our plumber for the day
leaves for the four-hour drive home
with a rifle on his lap
hoping for bush turkey, kangaroo.
There's a horned cow in town
going from yard to yard
in search of that grass
we keep seeing out beyond the town
at the horizon's edge.

Man in the Shade

Do you see that man
sitting in the shade
outside the shop
his wife next to him
and his grandchild
playing in the tree
behind him
do you see him
wearing the grey shirt
he wore yesterday
rolling himself a smoke
out there in the shade
outside the shop
do you see that he has
a phone and a pad and pen
on the table in front of him
and do you see he talks
to anyone who comes
up to him
well he's the Centrelink Office.

Waterthoughts

The woman who weaves baskets
from desert grasses
and likes to stand
in front of the air conditioner
with a cool drink on a hot day
invited us today
to go to the lake with her
on the weekend,
where she can help us
with the ceremony
that will make it possible
for us to swim in the lake
safe from its deep serpent
and we said yes,
if it's water and if it's a lake
and we can swim in it
and we can get there
without being bogged
we'll go with you.

The young heifer that
walks around the town
looking for water
came in to the school
as the sun came down today,
swinging her tail
and tilting her horns at us
as if to say
if there's water here
and if I can get to it
and drink it up

you won't be stopping me
not even that teacher
waving a stick
looking as if she wants me
to believe
she does this scaring of cows
every day.

Where is the Beginning of the Story?

She knows that every story
starts with that thin, proud
letter 'I', even the ones that don't
because if you look long enough
through the long grass of any text
you'll soon find an I standing up
above everything else
announcing itself as a beginning
then later the usual swarms of them
like grasshoppers across the rows
and paddocks of prose
the teacher asks her to read

so she runs her finger through
the seedy heads of the words,
parts them carefully, and points
to the beginning of the story,
there it is, 'I ......'
and she's right, the story does
always predictably start just there
even after a few false starts
because it can't start anywhere else.

Two-Hill

Today we walked up one
of the two hills
and looked across at
the other hill.

It had an eagle above it,
a row of rocks like a broken crown
at its top,
and below plains of tussock grasses
some good to ease the pain of teething
some good to give seeds for flour
some to give oil for healing sores
some good for baskets
some kinds a sign of water near
and some good for the shafts of spears.

Today we stood at the top of that hill
and discovered
we had mobile reception.

Sand Frog

Notaden nichollsi

Imagine a frog
small enough
to fit two or three
on your palm,
a sleepy-eyed, warty
plump as anything thing
and now imagine
digging out that frog
(kronk-kronk-kronk)
from its hole in the sand
and cooking it in the coals
of your fire
and then eating it—
and your cold going away
your headache too
and your skin looking
healthy again
and your eyes come to life.

Invisible Work

Ten of us crammed in
behind two propellers
with the pilot
eating his slightly odorous lunch
from his Tupperware box.
Earplugs in all our ears
and a world below
done in serpents of purple
clay coloured patches
stripes of dull ochre
then somehow bright green swathes
jagged hill-nubs
shrugged out of the heat
trees spreading out
like a panicked herd
across a plain
or gathered round a blue lake
its rivertail lost in meanders.
We land at Billiluna
(red sand a cushion for us),
Ringer Soak
(stonier, rumbling under us),
Halls Creek
(tarmac, perfect),
and finally Broome
(beside its great lump of sea),
and each time we land we pull
the yellow ear plugs out
as the pilot opens his window
to get a better look
through those invisible propellers.

Sleeping Crocodile Schoolyard Game

Today, play-acting the playground crocodile I caught
two children too slow on the flying-fox
in the jaws my stiffened arms had become.

Meanwhile a sleepy frog was chased out of the grass
under the wheel of a moving bin;

one girl found a finch and carried it,
limp, to her teacher.

It's important the crocodile's asleep when a child
launches herself out on the flying fox.

It's important each child gets a turn to hope it's possible
to slip past me the slow waking crocodile whose bite is so clumsy.

Desert Sonnet

Red sand spits grasshoppers into the air.
Frogs burrow into earthy hollows.
Even snakes keep out of the sun.
A child sings the alphabet,
getting it right. Another reads about
a clown with coloured balloons in suburban rooms.
At midday wire fences droop.
I walk, hatless, to the shop, and at the door
where panting dogs lie on the step
asleep in their bliss, a woman from the shade
across the way calls, hey it's closed, that shop,
and it is. As usual. I just forgot.
Walking back
I cannot get the alphabet out of my head.

News from Home

We hear of a mice plague in Fitzroy,
the cats too sleepy to chase a thought.
News of new ways of counting
out the unemployed.
We watch a Cardinal squirm in a Roman court.
He understands, he says,
his Church has lied to him about its heart.
A plane brought in grey bags of mail today,
subscriptions, brochures, cards and books.
At night boiling rain, the sand lightning lit.

Old grinding stones embedded in the desert;
the boys here know which hills are bushmen
and which hollows once were dingoes,
why the lake's so blue, where shells have gone,
who culled the horses,
and which team might win the weekend game
Mulan or the Halls Creek boys—
they'll play until the home team wins.

Children tell of what they know about
the pelican, emu, snake, it's the kind of news
that takes years to insinuate itself
far enough to feel like understanding.

Today, Unlike Any Other, Like All Others

No fresh food in the shop today,
supply truck bogged on the track
between Billiluna and Balgo.

Graders are coming in from
both directions to dig it out
before the lettuce wilts,
before the new milk sours.

Ian's fitting phones to houses,
wanders round the town
twisting old tele-wires together,
chatting to anyone who comes along.
He's a communication expert.

The earth today a damp red cushion
after last night's world-ending
convulsion of wind and rain.
Why didn't those few last trees snap?

The shop door dogs look soaked.
My dog, one child says, it doesn't have
a name, oh yes, it does have a name,
its name is Goodbye.
Goodbye? Your dog is called Goodbye?
No, it's Kunjia, Kunjia
the one who hid from the storm in the night.

Ways of Flying Out of Here

You could join the passing angels at night.
You could transform into a midday eagle.
You could be taken by the flying doctor
to join others considering mortality from the sky
or you could fly shakily to a holiday destination
in a single propeller plane too light to puncture clouds.
You could jump on the blue and silver mail plane
to lie down with the parcels, your head
on the flying, yearning letters of the lonely.
You could be taken by several planes
on a hopping journey to a place in a city
where you might find yourself at night dreaming
of a red dirt gravel airstrip in the scrub
lined by plastic cones and termite mounds
just outside a happenstance of homes
that you remember felt like home.

A Creation Story Every Night

Something big breaks apart out there.

Something unimaginable is thrown down.

The sky is blasted into the air.

The earth's spine takes this rain across its back.

A black and white dog flinches and flinches again.

It's the sound of ships falling out of the bottom of the sea.

Iron earth waking up, face down, smothered by itself.

What is Coming

The Minister is coming, they say—
a storm too, this wind its rumour
running ahead of it.
The Minister, they say, wants to
land his private jet here if he can.
Last week one tiny plane managed
to bog itself in the airstrip sand.

The coming storm decorates a sunset
in ripped-up gothic clouds of greys
and blacks. It's definitely coming.

The Minister, who's also coming,
will come with a bag of money,
(which government is he from?)
though no one can remember
applying for the money he's bringing.

Day's end children jump and laugh
on a sagging green tarpaulin tied
over an old tank until they're shouted
down by parents, back onto the blushing road's last heat.
(I understand their desire for bare feet.)

Looking forward to whatever
the storm will leave in its wake,
we drag shadows like sheets over ourselves at night.

Twelve Mothers

Every death, I read, has its echo.
Tonight the night ground is warm.
A car door slams on a shadow.
Twelve mothers in a circle, children
Drift like light through their laughter.
Technicians bent over their numbers
Decipher from the glow a final answer
Where we hear only low insistent hums.
Our visitor falls out of his narrow bed.
Every death joins hands with the past.
Children sing their songs inside a shed
Happy to be heard across the grass.
Doors are closed, windows glow.
Every death is a leap, we know.

Lost and Found

Termite mounds dotting the oval
Locks on every door and window
Hey you, yes you, are you the philosopher?
Cockroaches that live it up at night
A car groaning over something
Which of the prayers will stick?
Books appearing in the library at last
Computers considering access
Padlocks glittering smugly on gates
Electronics—spoken as an explanation
A forgotten question I meant to ask
A phone somewhere finally answered
Frogs lost in the grass and sand
Water pipes leaking happily together
Do you work here? Where?
Dogs looking for children's lunches
Finches at the leaking pipe, singing

A Brief History of Rain

Stones shine like lost buttons
On tracks gone soft and pocked
A rocky outcrop gleams dully
We go unnoticed by the weather
As some other slower story
Moves through and beyond us

A woman swings her arms
It's all that can be done

Grasses lean together, overcome
The sea will come as surely as it left
The present stretches
Across the road to the tree to the poles

I hear an army moving into position
Somewhere out there
Everything settles to getting soaked
Daylight glitters off each drifting drop
I wait impatient for time to have a go

at making history—
A bird's already talking about it out there
A dog's already announcing it from his yard
A man in a yellow t shirt wears a message out

The Three Little Cautionary Pigs

were so optimistic
when they set out
and so underdressed.

I want to be that one
in that red jacket, she said.
So we hurried through
the straw one and the stick one
to the brick one.

Is your house made of bricks
I asked her.
No, she said. There are no
bricks in this town and no
chimneys either. No wolves.
Only one pig called Daisy
living in a cage behind a tin house.
There are dingoes.

The bricks, the wolf, the sticks,
the fire, the chimney, the pot,
none of this can be the point.

Those three little
wolf-eating pigs
were so optimistic
so young
when they set out
and look, they built houses
like natural tradesmen
though those bricks, that straw and those sticks
couldn't make the buoyant boat
that was needed.

Time

Strange, this thin path
of our daily walk
across here,
dusty trail of footsteps
stones kicked aside
a diagonal meander
of foot-smoothed sand
across the school oval
skirting the court
and that tree
this faint and crooked scar line
its looping shape
echoing the gait
of someone walking
head-bent
across here
just now.

Pencil Grip

At first she holds it correctly,

then her forehead comes down
to the pencil's end
till she's pushing it around
with her forebrain.
Easy to let the end slip
into one nostril
for a more delicate manoeuvre.

Her hand shifts to hold it
like a digging stick,
a wand, a baton,
it can be anything
and almost is
as the sentence emerges
from her tiny storm

its words scorched across the paper
as if finally scratched out with the tip
of a lightning bolt.

Look at Me Skip

you keep the rhythm
and keep in one spot
as you jump, jump, jump
at first—
while the ones holding the rope
they watch and marvel
as they count your jumps
until your breath begins to fail you,
your calves and thighs burn
and your knees they wobble
and you begin to doubt that the rope
will slide beneath your soles
and clear your head every time—
oh, it was so easy at the beginning,
and now it's like a sentence
that won't end and still won't end
unless you find a way to stumble
       ungracefully
              out of it.

Never Quite That Far

We take turns on the ride-on mower.
It's our recreation and our therapy.
The fierce little engine becomes all there is
as rider and mower spit those twitchy grasshoppers
out of the way with dust, stones and twigs,

spinning round struggling trees that drop
a thin shade on the mowing mind.
It's more repetitious than the daily news,
evidence of work done to be done again
as long as Tony keeps the spark plugs clean
and the earth gives up its rain to the grass again.

The desert silent to its ringed horizon
nurses its hurts, counts its scars, settles for this
strategy of infinite blue indifference overhead
and a Martian puzzle of rocks and ridges out ahead.

Its our therapy and recreation,
We've set the sharpened blades so that
our shadows are cut sharp on the earth-red paths
and iron stones all the way to the further boundary
of school and town, road and hill—not quite as far
as you can see, no, despite our needs, never quite that far.

Toyota to the lake, Easter Sunday

Kestrels follow us, the whistling kestrel
and the black kelstrel too.
Their twiggy nests balance
in skeleton trees we pass
as a priest drives us through this desert
over scented herbs and seedy grass heads,
through creeks and boggy lake edge pools.

At the lake the women paint lake mud
on our faces, necks, arms, legs. The serpents watch.
The mud will keep us safe from them.
The kestrels hover like spirits
asking questions no one's answered yet.

We swim in the lake like worshippers and leave
dripping lake water on our laps and feet.
The kestrels keep to the heights
until we bog hopelessly in mud
that the distracted, blessed priest drove us into.

The kestrels settle on their trees
and watch us falling to our knees
chaining car to car in the hope that
by some miracle wheels would grip
so life could take its usual course again,
where the shadow of a kestrel crossing the yard
in the morning would be the ordinary morning.

Blue

I interrupt cockatoos chatting by the back fence.
They say something curt, possibly dismissive
and slip away to a neighbour's tree.
The door to the library won't keep quiet,
it cackles and shakes as if every opening is a joke.

At dusk a brief storm shoulders every tree in town
like a drunk weaving home through a crowd.
The day hurries away across grasses,
sand, stony rises, already beyond reach.
Lightning shows how broken the sky can be
despite all that shining blue polish lavished on it.

Bonfire Afterwards

The book of poetry I read today
had an old paint tin under a fence,
a dead snake by a verandah,
part of its boundary fence collapsed under
a fallen trunk, some rubbish in its far corner
beneath a wattle tree, two bird baths,
a rising sun, a forest path, several lovers and

a growing pile of cut grass, logs and branches
readied for the bonfire that will be lit
once the poems have been properly read,
highlighted and returned to the shelf.

The Blind Lice Snake

feeds only on lice
and can be placed
in the hair of a child
where it will eat the lice
on the head of the child
and not know ever
what kind of universe
it is
that brings
these surprising feasts.

Everything

You can't tell at the outset how much of everything
will be enough.
A mechanic down the road worked
on the town grader all day.
The louder his heavy metal music played
the better the engine of the grader went.

We walked in the dusk towards
the town's generator that goes unceasing
loud and hard behind its wire fence.
We passed a house with a beat box out front
and fairy lights too. We saw a pig, a cow,
and five children doing cartwheels.
We passed a house with the name Eugene
written across the front wall.
Later we could hear that grader moving
slow and loud through the night.
We turned for home. The horned cow watched us.
The children melted back to parents, aunts,
uncles playing cards or talking of the past.
This seemed to be enough of everything for one day.

Naming

W. H. Auden reported he was told
by a friend to take up poetry.
Upon reading some, he thought it seemed
achievable and mysterious enough.
He thought it
a bit like falling in love
with the name of a rock
—zircon or uranium,
instead of wanting to know
the rock itself, a way of keeping
in mind that *the child hiding in the*
shadow of a house with a lizard held
loosely in his soft left hand is not a
description of something, it is the
proper name of that child and the
name of the experience of meeting
that child in that shadow.
When I asked the child his name
he searched his memory and his
vocabulary, and looked down at the
lizard moving on his palm and at his
smaller brother whispering into his chest,
and said, eventually, D—.
Do you live here, I asked him.
Live here, he said.
He looked at the lizard again, his brother
whispered up at him again, he looked
around at the grass, the shadows, the
bright desert beyond us and almost said yes.
His brother pointed to another pale
sightless looking creature in the grass.

On Looking into a Dictionary of Walmajarri Words

There is a word for staying at home
when others have gone out—*yarti*
and close to this state of quiet being
are *yaru* and *yatu,*
the words for slow and softly.

The word for belongings is *ngari*
and the word for woman is *gnarinka.*

Tuparnu can be the swelling of a corpse
or the rising of a loaf.

A termite is a shadow man
and the word for chest,
tukurtuku
makes you feel as proud
as a little budgerigar singing when you say it.

Hills Beyond the Football Oval

Sitting on the roof of the Toyota
around us the few local hills
worn down to their gums
and bones in an endless solitude
bare themselves to a retreating sun
as if they can't get enough baking
in this pinging air.

Footballers slide in the dust and dodge
each other like airy ghosts.
They're dragging shadows as long as pythons.

Sitting on the spare tyre on the roof rack
I get photos of them racing past me, flying.

The hills ignore them
for the hills have a bigger story to attend to.

Pause

With silence comes
the low sound of distant machinery
in the ear
like a tiny freeway in there
or perhaps like the engine of a plane
whirring from cloud to cloud
across some inner sky.

Birds go past chirping small sentences
about insects and seeds,
with comments
on the welcome shade within a tree.

Time tucked away in a back pocket
holds its breath and closes its eyes
to the fear
it might never get going again.

My hand goes out to the ignition.

Finch

Finches of anxiety loose in me.
Cockatoos of camaraderie ignore me.
The high bird of prey can smell me.
Those finches they flit around inside me.

If I lie down they might settle somewhere.
Who knows, they might not. They want
to be everywhere and do everything
once they're awake like this.

Children charge at a swimming hole,
Cockatoos, contemptuous, pretend fright
and the high bird more silent than expected
is cursed by its shadow.

I want those finches to go
to the birdbath I've prepared for them
and drink there and dream of a place
where flight won't carry their fall so far,
a place where all that flitting will not fit.

Morning

At seven o'clock they come in by the gate
sleepy headed, uncombed, bare footed,
walking as if they have walked all night
to get here.

They are preparing themselves
for a day in Standard English
at tables where the future might open
one eye and look at them
with something like a promise that says,
yes, it is possible to live
several lives at once and to walk around inside
each one of them like some Adam.

Driving to the Nearest Town

I didn't know the radio was on until
I stopped the car fifty minutes later.
A world of metal borne against metal
had filled my ears as car and I thumped
across baked corrugations
like a couple of mad old bush turkeys
who'd lost their feathers decades ago
and every other part some dodgy prosthetic
made of tin stuck with bolts and chains
to hold us together more or less.

I kept looking in the rear view mirror
convinced I must be leaving half the car
on the road behind but all I could see
was red dust chasing us wild as horses.

Oh

The usual molten sky-swept cloud-curtained
nitid-black and zircon-blue brush strokes from that
most careless-fierce and lustrous artist in the sky
again today at dusk stopped me in my tracks
for, oh, twenty seconds.

What He Knows about the Tiger

He knows each part of the roaring yellow tiger:
nose ears whiskers teeth and tail
until we arrive at the stripes.
What those? he says.
Stripes, I say.
Stripes, he says.
Stripes, we agree.
Tomorrow we will make
this agreement all over again
unless that tiger would bring its stripes
into town in the night and swing its striped
tail through the air and drool stripes of mucus
from its meaty mouth at his door, its eyes striped
by the shadowy bars of knowledge glimpsed.

Inventory

these are my keys
one each for bicycle
car and house
this is my notebook
of patient pages
this is the pen
I worry about losing
and with it the pencil
that goes with eraser and sharpener
this is my wallet of plastic cards
that relieve others of fears
I might be an imposter
this is the shoulder bag
that goes everywhere with me
this is the place in it where
my phone slips in
never far from dying
there is a place for mints
and fading flimsy creased
receipts at the bottom

On reading a Book about Willy the Wimp

So, what is a wimp?

They look back at their teacher.

A carrot! someone tries.

I suppose, the teacher says, if a gorilla can be a wimp
a carrot can be a wimp.

But tell me, what is this wimpy wimpishness
in a carrot or a gorilla who is a boy in a book?

The word spills breathy from the lips, an almost-stutter
that can't rise above a whisper.

Let the sound go though you like a grumble goes through
a pack of dogs in the night.

Feel it like a flock of parrots feel panic
lift their feathers in the night.

That wimp—go on, say it—that wimp is apologising again.

Cockatoos

They landed in the eucalypts, folding up their wings,
And bobbed, small miracles on those thin branch tips.
When two black ravens sat among them they didn't mind.
Talk went on in endless anecdotes and screeched jokes.
The ravens managed a laugh and a harmless smoker's cough.
No Halleluiahs and no Amens—it was a weekend off.
When I walked out under them they lifted like a choir
into the blue until it flickered white with the host of them.
They know their business is really elsewhere and their visit
today our reminder that it might be some feathery heaven
we find ourselves in, obliged to speak the tongues of prophets
sorcerers and sibyls for a new age of bewilderment.
They strip the trees of hope and leave us walking on their litter.

Nothing Happened

You're at the local tip in forty-degree heat
among its old cars, lost toys and busted fridges,
emptying the car of a week's rubbish.
The flies like you very much.
It's as if they're starved of visitors two kilometres from town.
You throw your last box on the heap at the bottom of a hole
in the earth. It looks like the world's navel down there,
that famous sworled entrance to the underworld,
a place denied to the living and open to the dead.
You climb back up into the borrowed car
and push its ignition button.
Nothing.
Nothing happens
the next five times you do it.
Flies are in the car with you, the heat too, and the smell.
Steve arrives with his own load of rubbish.
You go across to him.
He says he's not a mechanic
as he twists the car's battery connection.
The car comes back to life.
It goes as if it never stopped
all the way back into town
where you park it as if nothing happened.

Gathered on the Ground

Cockatoos have come for the young eucalypt leaves.
They fill the trees then flick themselves into the sky
in a parody of panic. Their joke is endless.
The few trees bow to them, it's what they've come to accept.

Many people have come in cars for the funeral today.
They'll come close in under an open roof
and their voices will be heard, trees will try to shade them,
the wild cockatoos will circle further away
wary of such murmuring numbers gathered on the ground.

Professional Development

Our instructor reminds us
Aboriginal people had no beasts of burden
so they left nearly everything behind.

At camp, what was on the ground belonged to everybody.
Personal belongings hung high in nearby trees.
We imagine suspending toothbrush, diary, phone,
handkerchief and comb.

She tells us
the rich are interested in who you know
the middle class in what you do
and the poor in whether you're friend or enemy

We learn
the rich eat beautiful food
the middle class eat what's healthy
while the poor must eat what's filling.

And in any case
There's always music
and its shadow, the poetry that falls from our hands.

O is for Orangutan

We read the alphabet, we sing it up,
and when 'I' stands for Iguana I can see that
she would like to eat that lizard
after gutting it and throwing it on a fire.
She runs a hand across its skin.
She has seen an orangutan, she says,
on television, killing monkeys.
She drifts from knowing
to wondering what world she's come upon
in a library of jungle alphabets, purple trolls
and brittle giants who fall from magic bean stalks.

The Orangutan, forest child, swings eternally
in its book between the letters N and P,
not knowing whether what we speak is true
and never, never to reach its cousin Q,
but always hooting out its O,
its song of deep surprise and woe.

Lake

The lake is blue.
Blue lies like a lake on the lake.
Grass stands up wiry
all the way to the blue lake.
Everyone mentions the lake
once or twice a day.
It's a blue shadow on the mind.
No one's thirst can be quenched there.
The old salty tongue of the earth is in it.
The sun peers down into it.
The lake's face shudders under breezes.
That whisper it makes along its edges
leaves a slim rime of salt
circling its blue dream.
Red earth reddens as the day goes away.
The lake lies low
like a child lying down beside a mother
who talks to her of the lake and the last time they were there.

Five Seasons

We are well into the *Wurrkal* season
not long after those green grasshoppers left us
just as the pale grass begins to yellow.
We've one more swingeing rain to come
blown in with that low sky-wide cloud

and then the *Makurra* comes in on us,
the no-feeling season of big fires we sit around,
when cold rain's a danger to babies and the old,
when black-headed pythons lie fat and juicy.

After that cicadas sing in the hot *Parranga* time.
Mushrooms will come up, salt wattle can be eaten,
a hot wind will blow as if from giant faraway fires.

Marrji is the time of thunder. Animals wake up,
come out, look around at land, sky, lightning.
They listen to what the thunder has to say.
It's about breaking and softening the earth.

Wuruwuru is the time of rain. You call it Christmas
and remember snow. *Wuruwuru* is river and lake,
giant frog, biting fly, fish coming, road closing.
It keeps us home all those days with our hearts listening.

They Did It

Yes, they break into whatever's locked.
They break locks and make a mess
as best they can, you know, paint,
food, it doesn't matter. Whatever
they find—Who are they?
It's everyone, I guess.
Everyone does it at some time.
Shop, school, art centre, donga,
teachers' houses, rangers, nurses.
Those girls there, six years old,
they've done it. I've done it.
Sometimes we tire of it
before we've even broken a lock
and got in —Trouble?
Yes, we all get into trouble.
Who doesn't? People are upset
with us. With them. With the ones
who did it. We all know who did it
when it happens and we shake our heads
and bring the law to them, what law
we have, what law they'll listen to,
whatever law's big and solid enough
to still have a fearful shadow attached to it.

Yard Dog

The dog in the yard has plenty of space
to play and run and gnaw on old bones
and leftover shoes. It's his own place
but all he does is, nose down, patrol alone
the boundary fence, grazing a shoulder
along it, dreaming of it dissolving in a shiver
of light and dust so he might go out where
other dogs have the tracks and open air
to themselves, out where children
who torment him can be properly bitten.
He's making a thin line in the grass
along the inner boundary of his yard
and a soft whining song
escapes from him as he swings along
clockwise, heading West then East
where he sees me in the distance move across
open land on the rim of a fenceless paradise.

A Three-Job Day

1

Two cars bogged on the edge of town
down by the tip where wrecks end up,
the young man tells us
more in gestures and looks than words.
Snatch-strapped out those cars cough back to life
and the young man's grin says enough for now.

2

We shuffle four desks in a trailer from
the Reading Recovery Room to the Library
to Lynn's lounge room to the Play Room
and those desks are now much happier.

3

She rings us.
Someone outside
is banging on her windows.
I walk towards her house and wave
my brave torch at her walls
at a scrawny feral cat that runs
from her verandah and stands still
in the darkness staring back at me
two bright flat indignant discs
then gone beneath the fence
done for now with leaping for those nightly grasshoppers.

From Here to Melbourne

Rain from here to Melbourne
Canada's forest towns on fire
every last thing sodden or melting

shivering children dream of a picnic
with jam and damper, hot billy tea
and cordial out by the oval

Rain from here to Melbourne
fires doubling overnight in Canada
the children's fingers on fire with cold

Everything sodden or melting
the shopkeeper bogged halfway
between towns

children dreaming of dogs
and jumping cows and winter frogs

damper will be soft and warm
the tea a black and boiling mystery
neon cordial summer light gone sugary

Rain from here to Melbourne
fires eating Canada tonight
children rugged up dreaming

of books getting up and talking
to keep a fire in them burning
to keep the soaking rain inside them

The One True Teacher

Here cars float down creeks and bump up until found
Snug between a spindly tree and some old umber termite
      mound.
The children kill every chicklet found alive in its nest around
the bright school's newly furnished, daily watered playground.
The crusty road goes hard again two days along after rain.
No one's free of sickness, no one's free of loss or pain.
You can't safely speak of loving mothers, fathers, family
or sanctuary when the desert hands its creatures up so easily.
Children still talk of their one true teacher, Miss Emma,
who walked them through the bush, took them in for ice
      creams,
told them love and fun were what they could have forever.
The moon is fingernailing back its place below the scattered
      stars.
We're falling towards ourselves tonight as we arrive at dreams
that hear the murmur of the wings of a fast passing nightjar.

Spirit

If there is a desert, if there is a spirit,
if there's something fetid in the bush,
if plastics will outlast us all and if cars
are the bones young men dreamed up
and left here in twisted, weedy huddles,
if the last frog doesn't know what's in store,
if the promised flood's on the futures market,
if dust is real and covers souls as well as sins,
if there's a desert with a city built upon it,
if there's a misted valley under every bed,
if graves were shallower and prisons deeper,
if the cows had really given all they have,
if this is all there is for now and ever,
if brumbies' nightmares are of being culled,
if the desert hears dying voices in our voices,
if there's a spirit then we must be hearing it.

A Day in Education

They tried to listen to their hearts.
They tried to reason with their souls.
They tried to tie the laces of new boots.
They tried to line up like a nest of ants.
They tried to read a sentence on the art of damper.
They tried on boots that fitted everyone imperfectly.
They tried to kick a yellow football into the blue.
They tried to be defiant and obedient at once.
They tried to understand the psyche of the Bunyip.
They tried to run around the building once for fun.
They tried to dance the dance they'd seen on television.
They tried to wash their dishes without cleaning them.
They tried to listen to their hearts on their wrists.
They tried to whisper to the silence.
They tried to knot a knot in yellow laces.
They tried to stand in a line like Bunyips at a barbecue.
They tried to do it running, then running backwards.
They tried to get the day to go their way for once.

Repairs

The tiles in the shower recess were repaired today.
Tony did the job despite that tooth aching in his jaw.
Never mind they've gone from ochre to dull grey.

The hungry mouse behind the wall is locked away.
Tony's tradesman's tooth is loose and sore.
The tiles in the shower recess were repaired today.

His dismal knowledge: the dentist is two days away,
And might not, when he gets there, be any good at all.
Never mind they've gone from ochre to dull grey.

The main thing is the hole's repaired and we can stay.
He knelt in dust, patient as a prophet before the law.
The tiles in the shower recess were repaired today.

The poor scuttling mouse never did intend to stay.
Behind that tiled-up wall we will listen to it gnaw.
Never mind they've gone from ochre to dull grey.

The buckled roads will rough him up all the way.
His broken tooth's a gap his tongue will explore.
The tiles in the shower recess were repaired today.
Never mind they've gone from ochre to dull grey.

Going to the Shop Isn't Going to the Shop

You time it for just after the fortnightly truck
and even then the milk can be a week old,
cream beyond its use-by date
and potatoes already spotted. Coloured ices
are still cool as children ask for scissors
to open them. Ngarnkurr's there, long-beard-man,
concern in his eyes—all that bush tucker
out there those kids need to know about.
He knows a twenty-year life in seasons
under clouds of cockatoos.
Out the back, Brian flicks a working finger at
the leaking seals on the wheels of our Toyota.
We learn about something differential from him
and we know now if we drive it on much further
we're risking the old truck's final seizure.
A woman with an empty purse shows everyone
a picture of her painting that's fetching thousands
in the city, while she wonders what she can buy
from this morning's fresh delivery.

Desert Spirit

Wrapping up and rolling up
her painting, Spirit of the Kimberley,
for a competition to be judged
six hundred kilometres away
I worry that the judges might not see
this painting's

stained concrete floor
where it was laid out;
the chipped cramped kitchen table
where two women put the last
thickening touches to each symbol
and to that holy desert bird;
the sounds birds made
in the sky all day
to urge the women on
a little bit long time more
to finish the appointed task
as each season does in time;
the long thin stick one woman took
from her white curls
to make the dots as fine and layered
as the stones outside;
colours embedded in stilled eyes;
its women bent over it in a patchy shade;
the hope that there might really be in this place
lasting strength at the end of an arm
or a shaking hand, in a colour chosen for its grace.

Yes, Let's Go

And it would be like making a line on a map
beside a blue lake, birds to the right,
late sun in our sights, new blood in our hearts,
water in the back, diesel, energy snacks,
two spares, ropes, other things. Hawks
circling above for today's sacrifice.
Mice at home skirting our traps, blue poison
tablets under the sink, doors locked,
secret cracks in walls and floors that let the desert in.
We could do it, pack, lock up, go
for two, three days up there, then across
here to there on that faint line that must
mean it's at least a track or a gentle dried up
bed where someone's creek once moved slow
beside the anxious trees and watchful rocks.

We are Here

They arrive in masks, carrying hoses and sprays.
Music, overalls, sunglasses, gloves, caps,
their van plastered with warnings of invasion.
They move in compact pairs swift silent
using a master key on houses then the school,
updating extinguishers, sterilizing corners
rodents might nose into, then leave like palace guards
before a revolution. It's as if they were never here,
their deathly legacy necessarily invisible.
Wasps, rats, spiders, frogs, snakes are stunned
by what's sprayed on walls and floors.
At home afterwards, wary, we stamp our feet.

End of a Blessing

and bless the desert snake somewhere in the walls
of the playroom listening to children cry

and the boy following his father down the road
walking just like his father

bless the fires at the ends of our burning fingers
bless whatever lives in the hollows of the coolibah

and bless that couch passing on a trailer
as if someone's moving in or moving out

bless the dogs that go like dogs through our dreams
homeless and wholly themselves

and the woman carrying a baby while a man carries a pusher
beside her, the true dust on their real feet.

Gone But Not Gone

This is to let you know
we found the mouse

it was on the floor
of the wardrobe
under the black hose
of the vacuum cleaner,
its tiny belly full of green poison
and its head once swimming
in a final mousy confusion
lifted a little
as if to sniff what cannot be reached

it was soft to pick up but still held
its shape and colour
furriness too
that told of a life of rubbing
round corners, squinches and shelves

yes, the mouse has been put out
into the bin in a plastic bag

a smell persists
in the walls and floor
and along the edges of one door

we hope now
to become so used to it
that it will disappear in time

Camp, Lake Paruku

We discovered one new galaxy
an extra planet and six ways
to light a fire.

We slept with stars falling on us
dreamed of bears in a forest
dingoes on the dunes
and one of us got to sleep
with the 8 iron by her side.

We woke to budgerigars
busy among the coolibah
and gangs of white cockatoos
parachuting in pairs to tree tops
where they groomed each other
as if to show us their other
less juvenile side.

We scared an orange banded snake away
until, bright creature from a dream,
it disappeared beneath our tent
or possibly inside it.

We left behind ants sand flies lake
the easy screams of cockatoos
the pale green life of budgerigars
among the open arms of sturdy coolibah
saying to them we'll be back again soon
with the gift of our fearful dreams.

Briefly

We are not fishermen.
We are not even gardeners.
But we can be philosophical
enough to reduce every task to questions.

We do wear sandals and the earth
stays biblically dusty under its old sun.
We know that under this sun
without water
we'd last for three days at best.

We are not fishermen
and no one has called us
to cast nets at the centre of a lake at night.

We cannot risk being kissed
by mosquitoes at dusk.
Our lives depend on this.

Gates and cockatoos creak,
tree limbs and crows too.
In the sun water stews.

We use testing kits before we swim.
We are not fishermen.
We know nothing true about the soul.

On burned-out ground between dunes
small trees stand in their poses of agony.
The long dunes glow in the last light.

Found

a green and yellow jewel beetle asleep on the ground
a Fantale still in its wrapper
words in chalk on a gutter
an eyeless origami frog
a book that began with once and ended with after
a crow inspecting the ground
a boy shouldering despair
a girl prickling with swagger
a fresh wholemeal crust in the playground dust
ten deflated footballs
two youths cutting through the school
a woman who says she can drive her car each day for a few
    minutes only
a boy giving slices of banana from his sandwich to a girl
    surprised
those two young men cutting through—
one carrying a long staff like a sword
sunlight splashing in a pastel lake
a girl fishing through a box of prizes
and another girl discussing consequences with the Principal
all this and the boy and the girl and the young men too
in football jumpers cutting through a poem's last breath
as it holds up a brief hand to them in passing.

'After this, I saw another angel come down'

Revelation 18:1

A pair of them drove through town today
in a slow white car, counting
each house, stopping outside
one to debate a fine point.
They bought mineral water at the shop
and did it again, driving back
past every house, an arm out
an open side window as they counted
each dwelling, shed, ruin, old rainwater tank
now housing wasps, burnt out shade and snakes
no one's bothered to count before.
They did not stay long enough
to count the dogs or watch the sun
make its own deep blushing exit,
no, they were quickly gone
to count the better sins in greater cities
from the cooling comfort of that slow white car
under a perfect sky in another of their long unruffled days.

Preparations

You swept the verandah for them.
You put more prizes in the prize box.
You displayed a new alphabet poster
and swept the floor again.
You checked your word cards
and all the while the crow
perched outside talking to itself
about creation, seasons, beetles
and crusts it thought the children
had promised to leave behind.
You sharpened pencils
and replaced the reading books
in their boxes while the crow
laughed at something it had just said
to itself in its tree.
You put out a word game for them.
You faced some books' covers outwards
for them, hoping they would take
one up and look through it and want
to read it while the crow went on
with a story of lost baubles, mainly blue things,
and its memory of the taste of milk.

Origami Day

Not frightened enough by the future,
not even by the future that's behind them,
not rattled enough by the road out of here,
the children somehow do come back
each morning when the school siren goes
and the day strolls out to meet them
with its pockets full of surprises.

Later they'll abandon origami frogs
in green blue and pink for some new
kind of origami paper aeroplanes
to shoot at finches dogs and roofs
as they leave the school again,
their bright planes darting and falling
around their heads like warnings.

Add This

This mob she says
pointing to twenty book titles
all this mob
I like 'em
I read 'em
they're what I like
put 'em in here now
yeah, all this mob
you know 'em
I like 'em
put all them names in my list
go on

After School

the five young boys came at sunset
with a broken aluminium can
of slowly turning Witchetty Grubs
dug from the roots of a bush
on a hill not far away.
They taste of butter, they said.
Mazza asked if they had ever
eaten them raw. They nodded.
Have you been sick from them?
Never, they said.
He bit one's head off, spat, and chewed
the white mass of the body, nodding,
yes, butter, and cream too.
The young boys watched him eat it.
They agreed, butter and cream.
They held those grubs on their palms
as if they were small, soft glowing angels.

Hands

there was a crow cut from shadow,
loose pages of cockatoos lifted from trees,

and a man hunting on his knees
the bright green bird in the woody hollows,

an emu on the airstrip blue and tall,
children dancing on tin and knotted wire,

a Nankeen Kestrel reading the land trembling on its gyre
—a flying ghost of the soul,

a tree out there in sand near the lake
—its blood-red wood ready to make

the boomerang if we could wait for the man
to return with the knowledge in his hands.

Number 7

This one here
wirimangurru
from it we make
nulla nulla
spears and kuturu
from its core see
from that hard core

for breaking heads open
you can break bones too
and when it cuts you
you crawl around
too sick to stand up

we take these with us
when we visit up the road
no guns no axes

after this one
you need bush medicine
or the clinic

shields too we make from this wood,
and when you find the figure 7
you can make your boomerang from it

Journey to Kirta

Geese float up as we pass.
The lake's green depth remains.

Eagles hunt in pairs on the plains
above crackling grass.

Scrub bulls mad on melon
lie somewhere near us.

Here the salt cakes our lips
as we breath the lake's air.

We step on brittle salt wattle sticks
that have been lying on this land forever.

At the Council Meeting

chicken and sausages are being barbecued
behind the shop.
People say their houses need repair,
their streets long for names.
That path joining two parts of town,
someone says, it's too dark at night.
Some children still don't go to school.
Visitors arrive over that hill too fast
and then they're among the children and the dogs.
We need speed limits along there.

The dogs, they like these meetings.
They lie listening to chicken and sausage grilling.
They'd vote for another meeting next week.
The Shire President listens to everyone.
His voice is low, nothing surprises him.
Every complaint is noted down in a large book.
There could be a clean-up soon, he says.
Barbecued chicken is passed around first.
Bones are dropped to dogs at everyone's feet.
Someone says again
the houses need repairs of every kind you can imagine.

The desert listens, dogs listen, crows repeat the message
and the Shire President listens
until the meeting turns to the business
of feeding the children.

Procession

Children settle to their books or run
until they gasp and laugh or lose their way.
Crows like middle managers watch everyone
and take what they can.

The sky can't brighten any further and will not burn.
It lowers small planes from its blank height
letting them down near us here.
We go to the planes, curious about pilots
and those who come and go with them.

Crows and cockatoos slow and solemn
as processions of aging bishops
pass the Jesus Hill, the school, the generator
and acres of ruined gaping crinkled cars.

Crows

are here in larger and larger numbers
going about their shadowy business
under trees and eaves and across the grass
or behind parked cars outside the shop.

They have one sentence they repeat
to each other in shades
of many degrees of meaning.

Finches keep away, cockatoos are done with us.
Brooding blue and grey about the lake
brolgas kayak steadily across the skies
in ragged gatherings of ten or twelve.

Swans and Whistling Kites keep their secrets far from us.
Children leave us too for a football game
that will take them days to play and come back from.

The crows will stay to shoo the dogs from bins,
they'll kick insects up, and march across verandahs
like inspectors sent to find us.

The Steps It Takes

Young men grow into their football jumpers.
They move around the town in pairs all day,
they know which trees are poisonous,
where the strongest clubs can be made,
how to trap corellas, crows, wild budgies,
which boomerang can break an emu's leg.
They'll hunt cigarette butts from your ashtray.
Their bare feet feel the stones settle in the land.
I see them pass my window going down
then back then down again. Sometimes
they return with a child in their arms,
a woman at their side and the world keeps
turning at its pace. The young men know
each step in the dust along this road.

Canning Stock Route I

We found the moon at the end of a valley
of broken shale and spinifex

camels in long grass gurgling
stringy sounds from lifted nostrils,

red-faced sand dunes lying with their elbows up.

We found the casuarinas standing up
broken barked, lost between millennia.

We found ourselves among the termites
working by feel and instinct.

We found the wasp, the feral cat,
and heard the scratchy chirr of a circling kite.

We found Colonel Egerton-Warburton's crossing-place
on his march from East to West,

tracks that long ago lost themselves
and cliffs teetering above their future rubble.

We made a fire, burned our fingers, warmed our soles.

The springs survived, the tyres too.
The sandy curves were tight as a wary bushman's grin.

Canning Stock Route II

The map was more or less misleading
about everything but latitude and longitude.
The days kept going at us, pursuing us
as if to ask if we were there for the solitude.
The moon got itself up early, silvering
our night with its thin spun currency
and insubstantial shadows.
We bent to our tents like saints in a desert.
We dreamed of moving across the land
just above the grass and just below the dunes.
We had a human shape
and the landscape seemed to know it.
We cooked for each other
and asked only that the moon keep watch on us.

Voting

What do the young men do at night?
They put on boots, we believe,
and climb some gates and saunter to
the vehicles that brought today's
electoral officers to town.
The boys get chased
back over those shaky gates,
they drop a torch,
a spray can of Lynx
and disappear until it's time to vote
in the middle of the following day,
when they arrive barefoot, sandy,
uncombed, looking for a pencil,
asking if their names are really listed
and how they're spelled this time,
and is there anyone worth voting for today.

How to Get Something Done

You talk a little then you talk some more
you wait for the crucial meeting to pass
then talk a little more   then press the point
but not too hard   you wonder who it might
be best to talk to now   and everyone's so agreeable
everyone so equally equal but they're not
you've been told   so you talk some more then you talk
a little more but not too much
you choose the place where you talk with care
until someone hears you talk
and they talk to you too   and gradually
the people around here that you talked to
know what it is you will want to talk about
when you see them
and so it gets a little easier to talk
then you talk some more but not so much
that it might seem you're telling someone
what to do   or even what you'll do
it can't be rushed   it needs this talk
this settling talk and something else
that happens round the talk   beside the talk
as rivers here form lakes that settle to their shape
and certain depth and salty life all their own

At Home

When the wind runs thin in the afternoon
and the sun drifts to a seeming pause
girls come bouncing a basketball
and knock on the door
to ask if they can use the court at school.
They're at home in themselves,
one wearing her jacket on her head,
all of them gone off striding across the sand,
bowed into a knot of talk
that could go all day
until they sit, stiff limbed, big hipped,
grey-haired, scarred with knowledge,
children and grandchildren round them,
and find themselves to be the sharp-eyed elders
of their world.

'You will have a miserable life if you do not get an education'

Marcia Langton, 27 June 2016

The books have gone home with the children.
The seedy basket grass has been collected.
The brolgas have been counted.
The boys have filled their bike with fuel.
The teachers have the alphabet on the wall.
Old people sift through boxes of old photos.
The salt wattle shield has been sanded.
A map of this place is up on a wall.
Twisted cars pile up outside the town.
What should the young ones do all day?
Marcia Langton says it blunt as she can.
Children go home with hand-made certificates
though some will be lost in the dust.
We go by increments, just as each day does.

What is This Picture?

If there were sand everywhere outside
And the days were always sunny
And nearly everyone went barefoot
And teenagers wore only shorts and football jumpers,
And women wore colourful cast offs,
If cars had children on their roofs,
And if the single local shop shut by early afternoon
And mail arrived only once a week
And each sunset outdid the last
And if birds would not leave
And no one collected the rubbish
And only a few seemed to need to do any work
And the evenings started early and went on
With singing and drumming around the place
And hardly anyone combed their hair any more
And even the school teachers let their hair down
And cooking on coals was what everyone did
And if there were a lake nearby where you could swim
And watch water birds in their thousands bob,
If roads were there for children to play on
And people sat talking in circles out in the open
Would you realise where you were?

Preparations for Two Weeks Away

Pack the car
consult the map
fill the tank
fill water bottles
stack CDs
get jubes and USBs
consult the map
make a booking
pack clothes
books, camera, hats
consult the map
re-pack the car
make a list
re-pack the patient car
watch local kites
do tight circles
sensing a departure
leave a twenty dollar note
on the kitchen table
for whoever
breaks in this time

Lullaby

Under this bush, here, you can find the bush potato
if you have a crowbar handy.

The brolga knows where bush onions nestle.
We follow to where she has loosened the soil for us.

The season of the black-headed python is upon us.
Its burrow goes through there beneath the stones

and you might fall down and disappear if you go too near.
You might.

You can sleep among the cooling mounds of the termite
below that big old moon polished for us tonight.

On Reading *Boys Don't Dance* with a Group of Boys

In this book children beam, grin, smirk,
sneer, groan, and mouths drop open.

Ballet is mentioned on several pages.
They learn to say it in several ways.

In this book there is a bully, a small girl
and her older brother, a dance teacher,
and a mother,
each with something to say, sing, yell,
shout or whisper.

Three boys read the book to me
word by word, each one of them
ready to bully another
by smirking or groaning
at any one of them who stumbles,
stutters or mistakes
taking for talking, miming for smiling.

I can see that this might be what they have—
a tolerance for each other's envy,
a rough elegance of grins and smirks,
groans on the seam of a common song,
a dance that happens beyond
us somewhere in their future.

Merciful

A boy lying on his back
in the sun
on the oval

his friends watch him
from the shade
pull his green top
up over his head

a passing man leans over the boy
and says something
the boy shakes his head
and pulls the collar
of the green top
further over his head

the man who leans over
now leans even closer
and insists

the boy sits up
shakes his head
pulls his top down
stands up
and goes across to his friends
in the shade

they play ball together
for the next hour
as if they have learned
something about
being merciful to each other

just by watching a man
lean over a boy
sulking on the ground
under a ruthless sun
and a departing day
and the boy finally sitting up
and the man walking on his way

Shaved

the boys arrive with heads half shaved
ears on display with tufty leftovers
last rat tails and sometimes
one side still down over one eye

the boys' new haircuts make them new
and suddenly better at games
at smiling
at preening and touching
the tops of their heads

they are blind with curiosity
about what has happened to their looks

Looking After Country

"See that track there, if you go down there you come to a stone that is very beautiful and very old and very sacred to us. A tourist went down there a few years ago and found that stone and took it home, down south somewhere. Soon members of their family were dying. Every few months another one died. There was bad luck everywhere for them. They thought it might be the stone so they sent it back to us with an apology. I put the stone back in its place, and I never drive down there now, I only walk, because I want the track to grow over. So tourists wont be tempted to drive there. I have chained the stone down with three chains. It is very beautiful, you will see."

History and What Came First

once his morning pie is finished
coffee
then more talk on the shop verandah
another smoke
an errand for wife and baby

once this is done
he takes us

out past wild bulls
fattened on buffalo grass
past grey brolgas serene
as off-duty ballerinas
past salt wattle coolibah
cockroach-bush and kestrel
to a white beach by the side
of a lake we must now imagine

he slides from beneath tree roots
a smooth speckled green egg shaped rock
like a joke or a trick

he says if you hold it
(see how heavy it is)
long enough
it will change colour

he shows us with a wave across the sand
the spearheads flints and stone cutting knives
the chipping and flenching tools
some transparent as glass
some bright orange in our hands

we are witness to what's left for us
to leave out here
with the ignorant bull kings
rolling and farting on their fine white sand
over shells and stones
as they press tics from their hides
while above them
the brolga makes flying look as if it came first.

A Place

Children shiver over canteen porridge in the morning.
I'm still dizzy from going out without a hat yesterday.
The Ranger talks of caring for his grandmother's land.
I forget to go out to the airstrip on time.
Thumps of a football being kicked at school.
Two young men in opposing jumpers walk together.
A boy says to a teacher, this place is sacred and that rock is too.
A girl puts too much tinsel on an Eagles poster.
The tinsel will stick to the verandah for months.
A boy writes in large red letters: Mulan Dingoes.
I learn Mulan is the name of a miniature tree.
Crows knock down our bins and kick our garbage
down the road with perfect contempt for it.
Later I read an essay on the hatred of poetry
and find in it, after all, a place for the world.

Audit

If I haven't built a table or a bee box
if I haven't mended a car or a broken arm
if I haven't farmed a farm or worked a factory
if I've suffered whatever mattress was under me
if children did as they pleased when I called out 'stop'
if every time I sang happy birthday I was off key
if my heart has always been a murmuring onlooker
if these black birds around town were my many souls
if I've unrolled columns of ant words
along fading pathways out of here
if the wattle and the herbs are made by dew,
and rocks, like me, really do stiffen with age
then this is all that doesn't need remembering
when someone places above me a single wooden cross
painted white and tilting westward in its sandy place
over an abundance of plastic flowers got from a novelty shop.

Land Claim Meeting, Gnurra Kayanta*

We found thirty plastic chairs
(it took two hundred years)
two lawyers came
as they've come before
with cameras and anthropologists

The cockatoos calmed down
maps were laid out on the basketball court
stones holding edges down on the concrete
people watched from the plastic chairs
talk was long and sometimes short
rights to come and go were mentioned

Old men's beards and young men's beards were there
women were there bending down to trace
promises in lines across the map on the floor
marking off a tiny nation's twenty thousand
square kilometres of desert that might never die.

One lawyer said their case was strong the judge was fair
and their barrister the best one in the land

She said the strongest rights—the right to say
who comes who goes who stays away
will come to them

The plastic chairs held steady
people listened
people talked calm and low as though
this could and might and even would
be happening in someone's lifetime

as though to come this long way
out here today
to say we want it yes this land
would find an echo in a court room
where the chairs would be solid cushioned polished
and the learning long and proud and far from knowing
how a laid out map ripples in a breeze
sand blown across it
a hunting kite square above it
each dune a line into the heart

*On August 10, 2016, the day after the above meeting, Justice Michael Barker of the Federal Court of Australia held that the Ngurra Kayanta people (represented by Helicopter Tjungarrrayi) possess exclusive rights to possession, occupation, use and enjoyment of the determination area, and the nonexclusive right to take, use and enjoy the water in any watercourse, wetland or underground watercourse in the determination area. Justice Barker noted that these native title rights and interests have no effect in relation to other interests [such as mining interests] to the extent of any inconsistency, but otherwise the other interests co-exist with the native title rights and interests without extinguishing them. Lawyers continue to press for a determination of full rights.

Wild Bull

Buzzing with itself,
rank as a devil's toy,
two ultimate weapons
growing right out
of its brain
tail thicker than a python, eyes black as time
maker of fibrous turds
and deep sand baths
sounder of dawn, night swallower,
shadow-souled
ash-black brand
on the yellow plain

Nothing But This

Brolgas move away from us into the ceramic blue.
Clouds build an attitude that doesn't quite materialise.
Sand red then grey then white, grasses stiff and pale.
Termite mounds surround us rising curdled.
The lake licks its lip while far out fish huddle beneath it.
Eucalypt-bright budgies flick themselves from shade to shade.
Pummeled by sunlight we eat lunch with ants and dust.
We surprise a late kangaroo out looking for something.
Fires to the horizon are deep bloody slits across the earth.
Later we'll say yes it was a day when nothing happened.

Questions to a Fortune Teller

Will the cockatoos go away
if we bolt a hawk-shaped cut-out to the roof?

Will the dogs always have serious business
to attend to across town?

Will this stop that
if we put these on this table?

Will the orange moon become my friend?
Will we read about the end before it happens?

Will the crumbling hills crumble to the plains
in someone's lifetime?

Will we ever be forgiven for dying like this?
Will the last ones leave instructions for the tools?

Quiet

We sit outside the shop.
One boy is there in a football jumper.
A nurse comes and goes, waves.
A man is there, his wife away in hospital
though with a relative in every ward.
A dog waddles over to look at us.
We have water, vegetables, two soft drinks
and a weak Telstra signal.
Two pre-school boys climb Jesus Hill
and dance their way down
over rocks to a sandy road.
One girl chases another girl across the sand.
We hear laughter above the unceasing generator.
Another dog barks at another dog
and the shop door closes
on a day when most of the town is away at another funeral.

But Not

Walaryirti Art Centre, Balgo

a room full of paintings
and then another room
full of paintings
and behind these rooms
a smaller room full of paint tubs
and an office where canvas
is stretched and prepared
and behind the room of paint tubs
behind the office of stretched canvas
another room of conservators
digitising images
recording stories behind paintings
thousands of them
a task that brings remembering
into the picture almost too late

From here

eight hours to the nearest dentist
nine hours to the nearest masseur
four hours to the nearest hotel
sixteen hours to the nearest city
ten hours to the nearest sea
four hours to asphalt
twenty-six hours to the nearest relative
sixteen hours to the nearest book shop
six months more to connect to the internet
four hours from a plumber
ten hours to the nearest psychologist
two creek crossings and eight wild horses
to the nearest church and police station
ten hours to the nearest optometrist
four hours to a supermarket
ten hours to the nearest barista coffee
a week between mail packages
two weeks between deliveries of greens
months between visitors
nine hours to a mechanic
and one minute to a spinifex desert unrolled to a low horizon.

Open Armed and Heedless

The plaster Virgin in her grotto has lost her head.
Her left arm to the hand's split, perhaps by lightning.
Her right palm held out looks unwashed.
She stands as if she's come to greet us
after walking desert tracks for centuries,
her heart kept open to whatever's coming,
her white robe cinched at the waist
by that brown painted line, her toes showing
below the pale robe's dusty hem. We imagine her
walking here from paradise to welcome us
at her grotto by the graves. She's lost her head
but not her purpose. She can't move an arm or leg.
The desert talks to itself all day around her.
Breezes brush across plastic flowers laid barely above the land.

Notes Slipped into a Pocket

We saw a long lake smooth as a knife
lying out in the morning sunlight.

We saw at one end of the lake, fire,
at the other pelicans and swans
lounging on the bright water's edge.

We saw camel footprints trotting past
the mummified carcass of a bullock
its eye socket still holding a patch of night.

We saw a thousand birds lift into the air
as if a god had waved a burning hand
across the lake to see what would happen.

We stood on pale cracked salty earth,
magpie geese in a wavering line above us,
blue mud below greedy for soles and ankles.

Here the dingo hunts and here trees die
here black swans sing their sonorous poems
humourless and endlessly curious.

The blind lake never blinks. The earth shrinks.
The sun will rise and rise until its fury's spent.

We have keys in our pockets, sleep in our heads
and a car in the distance smaller than a tooth

come loose from the jawbone of a beast
left kissing the clay for years and years to come.

Sunday, Stroll

She came back from the lake, mud up to her ankles.
I was reading of Saint Francis dreaming of a hall
hung with weapons. We had fire, bread, a billy to boil.
Brolgas passed on their way to the salted mirror.
Her clay-blue feet turned grit-red as we walked
along a track through spinifex past a windmill,
a tangled fence that once wired the country together.
Lizards ran ahead, grasshoppers bumped against us.
A kestrel pair toured for small shots of fast hot life.
On a smaller track we came to the old rock.
The rock said nothing and did nothing
but like a god or a bird broken into flight
it could not cease being its own bright dream.

Salt Wattles

They contort themselves to hold
shade in close and keep insects busy
on their barky skins. They want finches
visiting, grubs too that make their way
along the roots into their hearts and
nerves. They stand apart from each other
in shocked poses like asylum inmates
let out to dramatise their inner horrors
for a sunlit hour. Adapt, adapt,
each salty wattle mutters into breezes
that teasingly spin round them at dusk.
Adapt, adapt, they think and dare
not open their eyes.

Honey Ant Lesson

Children look at illustrations of ants
and report on which ones they eat, licking
fingertips in memory of those ants
feasted on in another place, over there,
not far, a couple of days that way.
When they come to the Incredible Water Strider
on a still pond, they say ducks eat them.
In sentences inched out of them, they tell us,
each word a honey ant for their teacher to savour.

Women Walking Past

When it's all over, as it will be,
I'll miss watching the way women here walk
through the day as if wading waist deep
in children or as if pushing through
a calm green shallow lake,
through all that would defeat them
if they lost their dignity.
I watch those women walk past and know
nothing in the infinite future will be like this.

Word

Naughty, she said, swinging on a door when
a teacher asked her what she was there for.
She took her teacher's hand sure
the teacher knew the story now
and surely would forgive her everything
because she understood.
The single thing each word is—hinged
and swung upon.

'Night floods us suddenly as history'

Judith Wright, from 'Nigger's Leap, New England'

The eastern hills are broken, burned, tumbled.
Blood-flicked lines of fire slit the night.
A boy inherits forty thousand stars.
His father's gone to Kununurra now
to work and live and maybe die. He's missed.
I have them in my hair, he says and laughs.
We read of how the lice will glue their eggs
to ropes of hair and live on blood at night.
The lice survived twelve thousand years of ice.
The eastern hills are broken, cracked and loose.
The night, a quilt, a tide, a turning thought,
a cliff-edge no one saw—we hear it sound
its hammer in the heart. The eastern hills
still hold their stories echoed by the stars.
A boy walks boldly into camp and asks
if he can take a toy, a ball, a game, or
a blessing's shadow home with him today.
The lice survived a fire and a flood with us.
The birds are swept up in the light
that leaches bones and withers trees. We have
this much now—the boy, the hills, the birds.

The Story of the Rainbow Serpent

You don't know if it's curiosity or boredom
that takes you to the door, the pathway
out into the day—

the day out there with children
round its blue skirts and red-socked feet,
a scatter of children kicking up sand

for cigarette butts, loose change, old nails,
anything that might be worth having
when the storm comes.

Will it come? Will everything be smashed
as the story says, and will the serpent
lie beneath their feet afterwards

holding its breath and broken teeth?

You don't know if it's confusion or purpose
that takes you back to your house
as the great sun presses down.

You step on a wasp before you go in.
A lizard darts across the window pane.

Cat, Fire

We drove an hour sliding through sandy curves
bumping across clay depressions rattling over
corrugations to a woodland visited by brolgas,
pigeons, hawks and a wild ginger cat that came
silent up to our fire at night and sat as if we might
throw it a fish or a rat. It came twice and might have
inspected everything beside our tents
beneath those insistent stars once we were asleep
out by this lake that needs no word for itself but lives
by names of clay, sand, wood, bird and tumbleweed.
We went there for silence though it was as usual unbearable.

Portrait

She sprinkles holy water on us
as if it's the water we need.

Sometimes she stands so close
I'm sure she has something to say.

One eye on me, one spinning round
the world, she seems to see everything.

She knows cleaning won't clean anything
for long or for any good reason.

If she asks whether you're married,
you must say you are, and well.

Persistence is neither blessing nor curse.

She will not take a biscuit from you
but a packet, yes.

You repeat your answer (about marriage)
as often as needed.

She is, you discover, the one who knows
what's happening around here.

I do not see her for weeks then she is there
finishing a sentence in my ear.

One thing might lead to the same thing
forever if you listen to her.

When she sprinkles the holy water on us
we close our eyes (glasses held behind back).

We are as blessed as it is possible to be
when she's finished with us.

The Book About Snakes

We learn that a snake can smell
with its tongue. We learn that a snake
could be immobilised
for weeks after eating a gazelle.
To drink, a snake must push its head
below the water and gulp it in.
We learn the snake can sense your
body's warmth as you stand
prayerful on a mountain rim
somewhere near its usual paths.
Its tail, we read, functions like a hand.
We have our backs to the open doorway.
The snakes are out there
learning many other things
about themselves today.

Cubby

When school was finished
they went walking in the bush
looking for wood and iron
to make their own place.

Without a plan
and without anyone in charge
they built a place and crawled into it
amazed and happy that it fitted all four of them.

One went outside a little way
to scrape the ground
for a fire to burn.
Another caught a goanna
knocked its head against the earth
and threw it on the fire.
They could have lived there
year after year together
if that big wind had not blown everything away.

Next

I watch them grow out of their school uniforms
not sure what to grow into.

We read about birds who fall from nests.

Cars here go round in the dust
gathering dust and losing bits of themselves.

The world in here and the world out there
are nothing like the world we know.

Nothing to do but wait for the rain to arrive
and the irresistible wind's remembered song.

My soul wants to know why I do so little
for its survival.

I watch the children growing out of school,
their eyes seeing puzzles, their minds alive.

The late day hangs a spangled cloak on a hook outside
as it goes away again.

No One Goes

In 1977 the last old couple came out of the Gibson Desert
to die in a small outback town. The doctor who set out
to find them and found them was worried they might be
thirsty because of the ten-year drought that hadn't ended.

He discovered they were very old and very much in love.
They had run away years before to be with each other
against their families and against all traditions.
Someone wrote a book. The doctor kept a journal.

People here, forty years later, see fresh footprints
out in the desert—a child, a man, some women.
No one goes to find them this time.

Christmas Beetles

The beetles whack themselves against the walls.
They come to die where no one grieves or notices.
The air conditioner breathes endless vowels.

Theirs are the many deaths no one recalls.
They come and die like squalls of promises.
The beetles whack themselves against the walls.

Cooling ourselves inside, their death appalls
our wish for grief's consoling practices.
The air conditioner convulses, stalls.

We stand in quiet in our rooms and halls
recording every fall their deaths possess.
The beetles whack themselves against the walls.

Who knows what recording angel scrawls
all this as death sets up its local offices.
The air conditioner emits its keening calls.

Believers all, they seek what death forestalls:
Christmas flights and hopeful herbal poultices.
The beetles whack themselves against the walls.
The air conditioner breathes wordless calls.

Reading Man

Spider Man lives in Queens, New York.
I read this in a book.
There were convincing illustrations.
He keeps his costume in his bedroom.
His identity is his secret, even though
we all know about it.
Goanna Man lives around the corner
from here (true) and Brown Snake Man
is in the ceiling of the playroom.
Dustbin Man comes on Mondays
and I don't know where exactly he lives,
though I depend upon him.
Corella Man lives in the eucalypt trees
at the edge of town. He has a lot to say
and his costume is the best one of all.
Which brings us to Reading Man
who wears spectacles and sits down a lot.
His friends make fun of him.
He spends lunch times in the school library.
He doesn't have a secret costume
and can't find any books about himself anywhere.

'On the shore of the wide world'

John Keats, from 'When I Have Fears'

We are so isolated here that every roof has five satellite dishes on it.
We are so isolated here that there is no way to repair broken cars.
We are so isolated here that everything we dump in the tip is taken
       back again.
We are so isolated here that we cannot take your wars seriously.
We are so isolated here that our small dear quarrels consume us.
We are so isolated here that even crows are tired when they reach us.
We are so isolated here that dogs and cows and corellas rule us.
We are so isolated here yet we ache for solitude.
We are so isolated here that we're sure you've forgotten us more than
       once.

Jewel Beetle Plague

November is the time for philosopher-beetles.
They come, miniature wise men out of the east,
across the sand, thoughtful, heads down deep
in some question that hunches and hardens their backs.
Our house is the problem they break their heads on
then fall down beside. Swift darting turru take many.
I find their battered-suitcase bodies scattered
round the house each morning.
They might have meditated for years
before making this assault on our walls.
Each pinging death is a death I fail to understand.
They learn nothing from the ones who went before.
Their task must be this blind piloting into the solid night.

Still Here

Friends send emails asking if I'm still here.
I am, I say, and then give a few details.
Always dust is mentioned
and something about
whether the shop is open or closed.

This then is to let you know I'm still here
and feeling very much that I'm inside
the skin of the here of here just now.
It's a rare way of being here and won't last
for long so it's worth letting you know
I'm here, yes, and haven't left yet.

Seeking us All

Apart from crashing the ride-on mower into the house today
And not knowing where Oman is
And realizing just how uneven one of my favourite poets can be
And meeting two men with the same surname 'by coincidence'
And returning a bag a woman left on the back seat of the car
And falling in love with a self-indulgent sunset along the way
I have little to report to the night that comes so swiftly down
       the road.

Young Man

You're with the young man.
His black hair goes cloudy
on one side of his head.
His mouth's ready to eat the world.
His eyes are ready to run from you.
Each long limb
is a wild vine left untrimmed.
He has bounce in him.
It might be his spirit
banging to get out.
It might be what he knows
but can't say he knows.
He's saying something now
and the words come
swift and whispered and thin
and frail as smoke at you
and you don't know if you'll be able to catch them.

This is the Time of Year People Ask

outside the shop, on a bench:
Are you coming back next year?
We say, yes, we're coming back,
and the talk turns to how much better
next year will be than the one that's
almost grown up and left home.

We go home full of the ways
next year could be better,
knowing in detail now
the ways this year wasn't.
Every year becomes a runaway child, we think,
and the sand still unstoppable.

The Tobacco Poem

Father said Mass out on the verandah
bottles of water near everyone
children moving like smoke among us
and behind the priest a small hill
of the oldest most twisted rocks
God could grow spinifex around.
Locals call it Jesus Hill.
A white cross on top crookedly
juts into a crayon-blue sky.
The hill has more ancient names
but people say it's Jesus Hill
as if Jesus spent a night there.
He might have. And if he didn't
he would have wanted to if he could.

It's a good low hill next to a water tower
locals climb when they're out of prayers and hope
so others who live here will come to the base of it
and call up to them, 'Don't jump, we love you.
It will destroy us if you jump! Come down!'
and somehow shaky though that person is,
the people manage to talk her down
off that tower
and they sit on Jesus Hill for a while
as if Jesus had performed another miracle.

The priest poured from his travelling chalice
and took out a neat pack of hosts
while women sang in their language songs
about forgiveness, mercy, creation.
I understood the feelings but not the words.

At the end we all shook hands in a sign of peace
before cups of tea and plain biscuits came around.

While we drank our tea Bessie, Eileen, Karen and Lulu
asked me if they could get a lift to Balgo
for shopping.
Four of the most important women in town.
I said yes, we'll take you,
go home, get your purses, wallets and bags
and we'll pick you up in twenty minutes.

We drove across creeks and through families
of wild horses to Balgo
to the lavish new shop built last year
with a government grant.
We stopped outside.
The four women sat in the car.

We have no money, they said.
We want tobacco.
Will you buy us tobacco?
I bought them orange juice and soothing ices
but they wanted tobacco.
We sat at a table outside the shop.
I said I wouldn't buy tobacco
even if it was my own children asking.
Tobacco will kill you, I said.
Yes, Bessie, said, it will kill me
but I'm not going to die tomorrow
so you needn't worry about how you feel.

Bessie said she'd never go home
until I bought her tobacco.
The other women watched.

Lulu did buy tobacco, but, she said,
it was someone else's money and the tobacco
was for someone else, not for sharing.
She kept it in her pocket.
I don't know how it happened but at last
we were all back in the car,
squashed up against each other,
breathing each other's wishes fears prayers.
All right, Bessie said, you
go this way, without pointing.
Reading her mind, I went the wrong way
then the right way.
We stopped outside a house
and got directed to another house.
Now it was ash they wanted, the tasty ash
from the peeling bark of the Wirimangurru tree
to make chewing tobacco last and give it desert flavour.

Another house, a black pig being hosed,
and a naked man, beard to his navel,
sitting on a blanket outside his home.
Some scraps of tobacco were passed
into the car, pressed onto a palm.
No one at Balgo had the ash.
More houses for more tobacco scraps
until we left town talking about where ash
can be found at this time of year.

Halfway back one woman said, all right,
now you must write us the tobacco poem.

We slid back into town on this promise
unsure what had happened, hoping for the best
and under no illusions about the power of tobacco

and poetry in this desert.

Next day I agreed to drive out for Wirimangurru bark
by the lake, and after two slow trips
through faint tracks among salt wattle trees
Shirley Yoomarie found the bark.
We harvested two bags of it to burn down to ash,
to mix in with tobacco for the good chewing.

It was nearly time for next week's mass,
with last week's prayers blessedly settled we thought,
until Shirley and Waylen came banging on our door
in the early bright morning
to tell us Shirley's purse had dropped
to the ground as she gathered that bark,
her purse with everything in it
that proved who she was at the shop and the clinic.

Back out through slow waking brolga
and nervous wild horses to the place where we'd been
and there on the ground, sparkling, Shirley's purse
as if Jesus himself had placed it there at our feet.

Every day after that, Lulu would say,
remember, the tobacco poem, have you written it yet?
Yes, yes, the tobacco poem, I'd say, I'll write it

though the words won't sparkle like Shirley's purse
on the sand in the morning light under salt wattle shade
with the startled horses looking back over their shoulders
at us bent to the ground as if in prayer over something.

Night Walking

Throwing our usual caution aside
we walked out beyond the house
right into the night this time
until we felt it on our faces
low clouds pressing down.
The horizon became a wall
we might never reach.
An orange glow in the distance
from fires or wars, who knows.

Lightning spelled its crooked name
over and over on its black slate.
Our torch lit nothing but our feet.

We looked up into some incomprehensible adult universe
we could never hope to be taken into.

Somewhere

The puddles on the way out were deep
but not as deep we feared.
The lake, we realised when we arrived,
was retreating
though there was still a mighty mirror of it on the plain.
The earth a pale crust at our feet.
Always talk came back to whether it would ever be better
to be somewhere else.

Got My Culture Back

for Veronica Karnpirr Lulu

Feet in the dust
End of a paintbrush in her hair
Something wrong with her knees
Won't get better now
Songs moving through her
Steady the voice and the heart

Nuns and brothers said
This child can't stay in Billiluna
(Even though that's where
The bush medicine had cured her)
She must go to school
Let us teach her to write
Teach her to read
To sew cook and clean
Stand straight in a line be quiet at night
That's what will please us

Her feet in the dust
End of a paintbrush in her hair
Bright skirt on a body slowed down
She can sit here all day in the shade
Not going anywhere
Talking of all that the desert can teach us
Painting her story bush potato and yam
Bush turkey and melon
Brolga scratching sand for the jurnta

Lulu sings hymns to the father
The bird and the man

Chases the ash and watches the smoke
Rise from the land
Learned her culture again
When she got back to Mulan
Sings of rain on the lake and the claypans
Cockies in trees and Kiki the very first star

In the makurra season
The mungily seed
Will spill from its pods
There'll be damper and tea
At Lirra and Kiji

Her feet in the dust
End of a paintbrush
In her wild old Walmajarri hair
Wind still talks in her ear
And she knows that long wind
On its way to the lake
Will never say no
Its moan is its prayer
That carries an answer—
The rain when it comes
Will make the land better
Again and again

Resurrection

We walked out to the cemetery
and looked back on the town
as the risen will do one day
when they climb out of these mounds.
They'll see in the distance
the high water tower,
the roof of the basketball court and a few houses
huddled against a vast desert.
The risen will try to remember who they were
and who they could bear to visit now that everyone is back.

Prodigal Season

The sky, so steady, high and true for month
upon month now becomes troubled and low
spitting out birds, roughing up trees, kicking at sand,
hazing the sun, spoiling to fight with us and the dogs,
the sky an aging rockabilly prodigal creeps back
to find not forgiveness but the usual
understandable bitterness on every side.
I can hear the rumble in the sky of some old truck
being driven back here to be left among the wrecks
that already line the tracks and circle homes.
It won't be hard to recognise the storm when it comes.

Three Dog Doorway

Three dogs lie along the doorway to the shop.
Five women sit on a bench facing the dogs.

We're all sweating in this heat
but the dogs look comfortable.

I don't feel comfortable about stepping over dogs
in the doorway. Anything could happen.

Those dogs know everything they need to know
about us, and their jaws are always open.

One woman says, that's my dog, that one, and she names it.
The dog she named gets up and goes to her

so I slip through into the air-conditioned shop,
the only place where no dogs are allowed.

The dogs know this.

We know they lie in a line across the doorway to catch
the drift of the shop's cool air

where technically they might be obeying
the one rule we have for dogs.

But are they going by the spirit of the law
when they inch themselves so close to breaking it?

Only their dog-god who sees into their dog-souls
would know the answer

or even whether such a question is possible
for dogs who think more like lawyers than angels.

It's okay when I step over them on the way out,
laden with oranges and bread and potatoes.

They don't mind this coming and going
as long as there's no trouble.

X-Ray

for KL

I can see
the steady effort the painter made
to put those dots of colour down

over and over each other all the way down
the human-sized canvas that a woman now holds
like an x-ray screen in front of her,

showing explosions of tiny wild flowers
inside this woman holding this canvas.

How much does the painter want for it?
the woman asks and I can't hear the answer

but I know that whatever it is
it's more than the woman wants to pay

and less than the painter dreamed of
when she painted this new galaxy
showing inside that woman.

Before We Leave

we splash through growing puddles to visit the lake at dawn,
go from house to house leaving tins and clothes and stories,
check the weather reports, chase a dog or two from the door,
take a last walk past the water tower to the nearby cemetery
where plastic flowers still shout joy and grief and love and hope,
then we're gone.

www.ingramcontent.com/pod-product-compliance
Lightning Source LLC
Chambersburg PA
CBHW021157010426
R18062100001B/R180621PG41931CBX00001B/1